Table of Contents

I. Introduction

Take up the White Man's burden—
The savage wars of peace—
Fill full the mouth of Famine
And bid the sickness cease;
And when your goal is nearest
The end for others sought,
Watch Sloth and heathen Folly
Bring all your hope to nought.

Rudyard Kipling, 1899[1]

To accelerate the Taliban's removal from power in Afghanistan, the U.S. has allied itself with a loose coalition of ethnic groups under the banners of the Northern Alliance, Eastern Alliance, and southern Pashtun tribes. This union provided a backhanded strike at the Taliban regime by re-igniting a ground war with only a modest deployment of U.S. ground forces. While the operation in Afghanistan falls under the mantle of "war," U.S. foreign policy has grappled with smaller engagements throughout the world. In many cases, these deployments reflected "important" or "humanitarian" national interests as opposed to "vital" national interests. Whereas operations in pursuit of "vital" national interests might clearly warrant the use of our armed forces and the accompanying risk of casualties, interventions on lesser grounds tend to divide the nation in debate over the requisite costs in blood and treasure. Consequently, our national altruism and desire to erase injustices from the world is tempered by an equally fervent intolerance for prolonged conflict and excessive casualties. Surrogate armies bridge this gap.

---

[1] Rudyard Kipling, "The White Man's Burden," *Rudyard Kipling's Verse, Definitive Edition*, (Garden City, New York: Doubleday, Doran and Co., Inc., 1944), 322. The poem refers to the relationship between the United States and the Philippines.

For the purposes of this paper, a surrogate army refers to a military arm that is integrated into the joint force requirements, but not specifically a part of the joint force. It is a departure from traditional coalition forces in which a foreign army augments our deployed ground force. In this context, a surrogate army becomes the ground force of choice, filling the gap for a critical component of our military power that the National Command Authority (NCA) has opted to leave behind. Surrogate armies are a means to extend our war fighting ability into theaters or dimensions where we may be otherwise reluctant (for military, diplomatic, or political reasons) to delve. Recent operations in Kosovo and Afghanistan highlight the evolution of surrogate armies into a new paradigm and demonstrate the effectiveness of the symbiotic relationship between a surrogate army and her sponsor. To this end, the U.S. armed forces must embrace surrogate armies as an extension of foreign policy that extends beyond the doctrine of our joint and special operations forces.

This paper will briefly examine the evolution of U.S.-backed surrogate armies citing cases of both success and failure. It will examine our current doctrine and establish that there is, in fact, a new operational paradigm. Finally, it will define the conditions that would warrant and best be served by a surrogate army in our current global environment, identify potential pitfalls, and offer suggestions to mitigate their shortcomings.

II.   The History

The mere absence of war is not peace.

John F. Kennedy
1963 State of the Union Address[2]

Elements of surrogate forces can be found throughout our history. In early America,

colonial powers depended heavily on Native American forces as the Europeans expanded their

empires and waged war through these surrogates. The Cold War superpowers refined this

warfare tool through proxy wars and insurgencies, attempting to promote their agendas

through a shell game of indirect conflicts. U.S. attempts to shape international politics through

this dimension of military power have had mixed results; even so, they illustrate four pervasive

themes which become the precursors for choosing surrogate forces.

First, the U.S. should avoid becoming embroiled in ground conflicts seeded by

religious, cultural, or ethnic enmities. The Soviets learned this through their experience in

Afghanistan in the 1980s while the U.S. received a taste of it in the Balkans a decade later.

The U.S. armed forces, while skilled in executing military tasks, have been less effective in

solving problems rooted in these areas.[3] Conflicts of this nature become prime candidates for

surrogates.

Second, the U.S. must maintain its ability to leverage the indigenous force or

government. In Southeast Asia, our excessive investment in manpower and equipment (and

---

[2] As quoted in Office of the Assistant Secretary of Defense (Special Operations/Low-Intensity Conflict), *United States Special Operations Forces Posture Statement 2000*, (Washington, D.C.), 5.

[3] Henry H. Shelton, "From the Chairman: U.S. Military and Foreign Policy," *Harvard International Review*, vol. XX, no. 1 (Winter 1997/1998): 77.

ultimately lives) eclipsed our ability to leverage the South Vietnamese government.[4]

Vietnamese domestic policy failures left a void that we attempted to fill through expanded military involvement. We were in deep, and it was difficult to get out regardless of what the South Vietnamese government did.[5] Ultimately, it was 10 years, half a million casualties, and 150 billion dollars before we were able to leave South Vietnam. In contrast, our success in El Salvador was highlighted by our minimal investment in manpower. Although we had made contributions in materiel and weapons, Congress had limited our military presence to 55 soldiers.[6] If the Salvadorian leadership began to stray from agreed upon goals, the American support force could be loaded quickly on a C-130 transport and flown out of country. This leverage will become essential to later operations employing surrogates.

Third, any surrogate force must garner the support of the population and be legitimate in their eyes. The military and government must be part of the solution, not part of the problem. These institutions must recognize the root causes of discord and address true reforms

---

[4] Direct U.S. involvement began in Vietnam in 1954 with a relatively small military advisory group. In time, however, our role expanded, and U.S. forces assumed an even greater burden in military operations. In 1965, we had 75,000 service members fighting in Southeast Asia. By 1966, that number had grown to 375,000, and by 1969, we had over half a million soldiers committed to the struggle. These figures vary depending on the source, these particular numbers were drawn from Alan Axelrod, *The Complete Idiot's Guide to American History*, (Indianapolis, Indiana: Alpha Books, 2000), 284. By the time the United States finally withdrew in 1975, we had invested over $150 billion in Vietnam and lost 58,000 soldiers in the process (Ibid., 290).

[5] It was a path the U.S. was heading down with our support to Chiang Kai-shek in China until President Truman pulled the plug on continued support. In this case, the magnitude of U.S. intervention and the probable costs were "out of proportion with the results to be obtained." (George C. Marshall, 21 February 1948, as quoted in lecture notes by Thomas G. Mahnken, "U.S. Intervention in the Chinese Civil War," Naval War College Strategy and Policy Department lecture, 9 October 2001). Chiang failed to institute land reform and reconstitute his own military forces to make the best use of U.S. aid. Further, he continued to tie ridiculous demands to his continued fight against the Japanese such as a billion-dollar gold loan to continue the fight. In time, the administration's feeling was that no amount of U.S. forces or aid could win the war for the Nationalists. See Edward L. Dreyer, *China at War, 1901-1949*, (New York: Longman Group Limited, 1995), pp. 284 and 320.

[6] Professor Waghelstein concedes that while this number of U.S. troops was quite small, it was sufficient to accomplish the mission. More importantly, our limited investment allowed the American ground force commander to effectively leverage the Salvadorian leadership. In general, he maintains that it takes between 60 and 70 trainers to effective train a battalion. See John D. Waghelstein, *El Salvador*, (Carlisle Barracks, PA: U.S. Army Military History Institute, Senior Officers Oral History Program, 1985), 102.

to win the trust of the people. To this end, the government must be committed and mobilize its resources to target political, social, and economic problems.[7] The South Vietnamese government failed to provide basic protections for their citizens, thereby eroding governmental authority and the credibility of the South Vietnamese army.[8] In El Salvador, this became the impetus for the villages to defend themselves. Once you have an armed citizenry that is willing "to defend each *pueblocito*, then you already have the war won."[9] The rest of the battle is a matter of sorting out the guerrillas whose popular support base will wither with in the face of a population armed against them.[10] The infamous Ernesto "Che" Guevara illustrates this phenomenon through his misguided, and ill-fated, attempt to export the Cuban-brand of revolution to Bolivia in 1966.[11]

Fourth, the U.S. must align itself with insurgents or surrogates with the will to fight and die (with or without major power support).[12] While we can ship weapons and materiel, we cannot generate or import a deep-seeded desire to fight. The Northern Alliance provides a

---

[7] Ibid., 31. Colonel John D. Waghelstein was the American ground force commander in El Salvador. He is now retired and is currently a professor at the Naval War College in Newport, Rhode Island.

[8] Department of the Army. *Operations*. Field Manual 3-0. (Washington, D.C.: June 2001), p. 9-16.

[9] Waghelstein, 32.

[10] Ibid.

[11] Che had misread the socio-economic conditions facing the populace and assumed that Cuba's formula for revolution would take root in Bolivia. The difference was, however, that the Bolivian government had already instigated true land reform. The people were happy. Che missed this and was seen as a threat by the populace. His popular support evaporated and, with it, his guerrilla movement. He was subsequently turned over to government forces and executed in 1967. Che's failed attempt to dramatically reshape Bolivia's government served to illustrate that "doing right by the people" is essential to a successful land campaign. This condition existed in Vietnam as well, as the United States, in its fervent desire to stem the flow of communism, turned a blind eye to the unpopular, impotent, and largely corrupt South Vietnamese regime.

[12] In general, successful insurgent forces require four essential elements: the willingness to fight and die (with or without major power support), the military capability to take on a regime's forces, the internal backing from a sizable faction of the population, and support from at least one neighboring state. See Daniel L. Byman, Kenneth M. Pollack, and Gideon G. Rose, "Beef Up the Taliban's Enemy," *RAND Op-Eds*, 20 September 2001, <http://www.rand.org/hot/op-eds/092001LAT html> [21 November 2001].

good example of this tenet. They represent a "homegrown movement opposed to a homegrown tyranny."[13] They are not the "local dupes for a foreign ideology" or, like the South Vietnamese regime, an "elite, corrupt clique of Catholics in a nation of Buddhist peasants."[14]

Collectively, these conflicts provided the military with a litany of lessons learned. Among other things, the U.S. has learned that sometimes we must fight without overwhelming force and that, sometimes, massive firepower is only marginally relevant (as in current anti-terrorism efforts).[15] In an evolving surrogate paradigm, our experiences highlight the importance of identifying a legitimate, indigenous ground force in cases where the U.S. stands to be embroiled in the convoluted environment of ethnicity and cultural differences. These surrogate themes gain increased significance as one considers recent U.S. involvement in Kosovo and Afghanistan.

III.   The Evolution -- Enter Kosovo

> *So, we did diplomacy backed by force, and*
> *now we're into force backed by diplomacy.*
>
> Secretary of State Madeleine Albright
> 12 April 1999[16]

NATO's war in Kosovo contained many of the themes previously discussed. From the onset, Kosovo was a volatile environment for U.S. troops, the roots of which were seeded in

---

[13] Michael Moran, "Uneasy alliance," *MSNBC Website*, 15 November 2001, <http://www.msnbc.com/news/657739.asp#BODY> [21 November 2001].

[14] Ibid.

[15] James Webb, "A New Doctrine for New Wars," *Wall Street Journal*, 30 November 2001, A14.

[16] As quoted in Wesley K. Clark, *Waging Modern War*, (New York: PublicAffairs, 2001), 253.

ethic and religious differences dating as far back as 1389.[17] Some 600 years later, the conflict was still muddled. In the Kosovo Liberation Army (KLA), however, there was a legitimate ground force with the will to fight in theater. This force provided an interesting, albeit unplanned, option for NATO's leadership and ushered in the shift to this new surrogate force paradigm.

The harbinger of this evolutionary progression was that domestic and international pressures induced the U.S. to exclude the critical ground component from their joint force.[18] In doing so, the U.S. found itself reluctantly adopting the KLA as a surrogate to fill this essential role. General Wesley Clark was largely opposed to arming the KLA and letting them fight. He did not see the KLA as a long-term solution, but rather a means of prolonging and enlarging the crisis.[19] Clark felt the KLA was a "halfway measure" that "wouldn't help much" and, therefore, should operate strictly as guerrillas.[20] Chairman of the Joint Chiefs of Staff

---

[17] The Battle of Kosovo in 1389 took place near Pristina and was a Serb attempt to fend off the invading Turks. With the fall of Constantinople in 1453, Ottoman Turks dominated the region. Muslim Albanians were seen as sympathetic to the Turkish invaders and, over time, Kosovo's populations became increasingly ethnic Albanian. By the late 17th Century, there was a large Serb exodus from the region. The Ottoman rule came to an end in 1699, and the Serbs, Macedonians, and Bulgarians drove them out of the Balkans. Serbia became a formal state in 1878 and took control of Kosovo with the Treaty of Berlin. See Ivo H. Daalder and Michael E. O'Hanlon, *Winning Ugly: NATO's War to Save Kosovo*, (Washington, D.C.: Brookings Institution Press, 2000), pp. 6-7. Although, unlike other former Yugoslavian republics such as Bosnia and Croatia, Kosovo was regarded as an integral part of Serbia and, subsequently, received secondary foreign policy billing by the U.S. and Western powers (Ibid., 9). The KLA appeared in 1996 and engaged in sporadic harassment and killing of Serb authorities. The Serbs, under Slobodan Milosevic, began to retaliate in force. By autumn of 1998, hundreds of ethnic Albanians had been killed with thousands displaced, and reports of Serb atrocities were reaching the West. Ultimately, 1.3 million ethnic Albanians were forcibly removed from their homes and another 800,000 were pushed entirely out of Kosovo (Ibid., vii). On 24 March 1999, after extensive diplomatic negotiations, NATO went to war in the belief that a few days of limited bombing would persuade Milosevic to end the attacks and accept a political solution (Ibid.).

[18] Even in the face of the military's advocacy of this option, the Administration feared that a ground war would be opposed by Congress at home (threatening the operation's funding) and by our allies abroad (threatening the coalition) (Ibid., 53). NATO Secretary General Javier Solana saw the ground option as a divisive issue and was opposed to bringing it before the council. See Clark, 166.

[19] Ibid., 343.

[20] Ibid., 342.

General Henry Shelton and Secretary of Defense William Cohen recognized the KLA's potential and informed Congress that the KLA might ultimately play the role of the ground force, allowing NATO to avoid any such role itself.[21] Overtime, the role of the KLA did increase. Despite their modest size, the KLA began to conduct limited offensives against Serb positions in Kosovo, which forced the Serbs out of their defensive posture and made them more vulnerable to attack. Additionally, they were able to assist in spotting targets and in reporting which villages were clear of Kosovar citizens. [22]

Unfortunately, the prospect of using the KLA offered unique challenges. As one senior Western diplomat put it, "We don't have leverage on the KLA. It is a missing element in our overall strategy."[23] Without NATO troops on the ground in Kosovo, there was nothing the Allies could do to prevent the KLA from taking advantage of the Serb's new reduced security presence. Cohen's attitude was that the "KLA was not going to use the NATO to serve its own purposes" and that NATO would not be "the Air Force for the KLA."[24] Outright arming raised the specter of losing control of a "loose ally." NATO recognized that the KLA's

---

[21] Eric Schmitt, "Legislators Told Air Plan Needs Time," *The New York Times*, 16 April 1999, A10, as quoted in Daalder and O'Hanlon, 115.

[22] Several challenges existed in this system. In many cases, the KLA information was old or not as accurate as required. Furthermore, NATO's relationship with the KLA necessitated the use of intermediaries to relay information. The NATO alliance knew the KLA's general patters of operations. Task Force Hawk was in contact with the Albanian Army who was monitoring the KLA. U.S. ground forces were not permitted to directly engage targets and had to pass the information to the Air Force pilots overhead who then had to visually search for the targets. This process resulted in many delays and many lost opportunities. See Clark, 329. This reduced the reliability of the information and increased the susceptibility of the communications to Serb infiltration (Ibid., 275). The lack of a NATO ground presence posed an additional challenge with regard to non-governmental organizations (NGOs) in Kosovo. NGO movements were uncoordinated and lacked communications. The allies did not want to bomb them by mistake and create a media firestorm, but they could neither block nor control the NGOs. Despite their good intentions, the NGOs became another battlefield hazard (Ibid., 277).

[23] Mike O'Connor, "Kosovo Rebels Gain Ground under NATO Threat," *The New York Times*, 4 December 1998, A3, as quoted in Daalder and O'Hanlon, 57.

[24] Daalder and O'Hanlon, 35.

ambitions extended beyond merely increased autonomy in Kosovo and were not shared by the Western governments or Russia.[25] There was the distinct possibility that a "self-confident and victorious" KLA might try to extend its Albanian triumph into other regions such as Macedonia.[26] Additionally, for NATO to be successful in its peacekeeping effort, it had to remain unbiased. Further, there was the pervasive fear that a drawn out guerrilla war would turn Kosovo into another European Afghanistan or Angola.[27] Consequently, these elements combined to give the U.S. pause in accepting the KLA as an ally and resulted in the U.S. repeatedly denying the KLA's request for weapons.

Even after NATO planes had begun bombing, the Clinton Administration and its European allies continued to debate the proper course for the war. Military leaders were hesitant to step forward and take responsibility for difficult and dangerous actions in what they regarded as a less than vital region.[28] Relying on NATO airpower was a possibility; however, Clark and his NATO counterparts recognized that they might need the threat of further escalation to successfully prosecute the war.[29] Milosevic always felt he could weather NATO's air attack, and without the danger of a ground invasion, his pressure to negotiate was minimal. The result was an incremental and reactive approach that required 78 days of

---

[25] The KLA sought outright independence, restoring autonomy was not enough. In the Albanian's view, they had lived in the region for centuries, were the overwhelming majority of the population, and had borne the brunt of Serb repression for years (Ibid., 37).

[26] Ibid., 68.

[27] Ibid., 16.

[28] Clark, 119.

[29] Ibid., 117. German Klaus Naumann, Chairman of the NATO Military Committee, noted that, unlike the Croat's ground campaign in 1995, there was no comparable force to threaten the Serbs with defeat. In January 1999, Clark had advised several senators, "if the air campaign doesn't succeed, then we have to be prepared to follow up with ground troops...maybe up to 200,000..." See page 168.

bombing (combined with the very real threat of ground invasion and Serbia's loss of Russian support) to force the Serbs out of Kosovo and allow a NATO-led international force to enter.[30] This impending NATO ground assault, real or perceived, was made all the more tangible through the persistent efforts of the KLA. [31] These actions demonstrated the necessity of a ground force in the conflict and demonstrated the utility of the KLA as a surrogate to NATO's Joint Force Commander. This lesson was not lost on the planners as the U.S. delved into the quagmire of Afghanistan.

IV.   Enter Afghanistan

> *We welcome the Northern Alliance forces because they*
> *are our people, not foreign forces.*

Sher Agha, a former Afghan army officer[32]

Some have referred to our operation in Afghanistan as a "classic" colonial war in which the U.S. uses its own troops sparingly while choosing local allies as proxies and accelerating their victory through our technological superiority.[33] As with the Balkans, Afghanistan is an unenviable environment rooted in ethnic tribal differences. On a tactical level, the role of the Afghan resistance is much like the role of the KLA.[34] The U.S. benefits

---

[30] Daalder and O'Hanlon, 17; Clark, pp. 405-406.

[31] Milosevic precipitated his own demise by departing from traditional counterinsurgency methods. His continued attacks on civilians further alienated the population and only enhanced the recruiting efforts of the KLA. See Clark, 108. By the end of the war, the KLA's ranks roughly doubled in size to 17,000. See Daalder and O'Hanlon, pages 114 and 151.

[32] "Opposition Seizes Control of Kabul," <http://www.washingtonpost.com/wp-dyn/articles/A20835-2001Nov13 html> [21 November 2001].

[33] David Warren, "America's Advantage," *DavidWarrenOnline,* Essays on Our Times, 12 December 2001, <davidwarrenonline.com> [17 December 2001].

[34] For the purposes of this paper, the "Afghan resistance" refers to the confederation of tribal, ethnic, and religious and other groups who have organized to fight the Taliban. It includes the Northern Alliance, Eastern Shura (Eastern Alliance), and Pashtun tribes. Many of these groups organized to fight the Soviets in the 1980s.

from a ground force in Afghanistan that is familiar with the terrain, climate, language, customs, and people of the area. We create a condition were Afghan fights Afghan, and our, sometimes obtrusive, ground presence is muted by an indigenous force that is welcomed by the local population. In doing so, we avoid popular backlash by a population that has long resisted foreign invaders.[35] Furthermore, such an army has provided a facet of access not normally available to our forces. For example, U.S. coalition troops have access to airspace in Tajikistan, which has strong ethnic ties to the Northern Alliance.[36] Resistance fighters provide a way to "raise the stakes" against the Taliban who have resisted years of economic sanctions and diplomatic isolation. The U.S., in turn, leverages the Afghan resistance with weapons, ammunition, supplies, intelligence, and training. Satellite telephones and global positioning devices enable Afghan ground commanders to request back up through air strikes and special operations forces (SOF) resulting in the evaporation of Taliban sanctuaries. Throughout the conflict, our surrogate Afghan fighters have proven to be a critical element of the "joint" force while never being fully integrated into our force structure.

As with our reluctant alliance with the KLA in Kosovo, the decision to support the Northern Alliance and similar fighters followed weeks of contradictory signals.[37] From the outset, we recognized Pakistan's importance as an ally, yet Pakistan has been embroiled in her own conflicts with the Northern Alliance. There was concern that the Afghan resistance

---

[35] Charles Krauthammer, "We Don't Peacekeep," *Washington Post*, 18 December 2001, 27.

[36] Both Uzbekistan and Tajikistan are part of NATO's Partnership for Peace and are forging closer ties with the U.S. Even in Iran, the Northern Alliance shares the bond of Shi'ite Muslims whereas the Taliban are Sunni Muslims. Consequently, the Taliban endures poor relations with Iran while the U.S. (even with our Iranian track record) has been promised protection for any downed aviators. Michael Snider, "A Quagmire of Alliances and Enmities," *Maclean's,* 8 October 2001, Lexis-Nexis, Dayton, OH: Lexis-Nexis. <http://web.lexis-nxis.com/universe/document?_m=5c0b8097f59ccee3991ea2eac70b46d3&_docnum =39&wchp=dGLStV-lSlAl&_md5=8f46711b35c0c99c9bb39afd261385cc> (21 November 2001).

[37] Michael R. Gordon, "Alliance of Convenience," *The New York Times*, 23 October 2001, A1.

fighters were no better than the Taliban when it came to ruling the civilian population. There was also concern that these forces would quickly pursue objectives contrary to those of the United States. Fortunately, the anti-Taliban fighters have proved to be disciplined and relatively judicious during the liberation of various Afghan cities. However, as will be discussed further, the war aims of the U.S. and the anti-Taliban forces do not always neatly coincide.

In spite of the challenges of operating on the ground through a surrogate, the U.S. has recognized its inherent advantages and opted to exclude a significant component of U.S. ground forces from the fight.[38] Instead, we continue to prosecute the campaign in Afghanistan on the tenets of lethal air and special operations forces and a ground campaign carried out primarily through indigenous fighters. How this operation plays out with our surrogate army remains to be seen.

V. The Doctrine

> *As far as Schwarzkopf was concerned, the "snake eaters"*
> *tended to exaggerate and get themselves into trouble.*

> From Gordon and Trainor's book, *The Generals' War*[39]

Beyond coalition references spawned from our Gulf War experience, our joint doctrine makes little reference to the integration of foreign forces into the joint task force and no prescription for offering a foreign army as the primary ground component in a U.S.-led

---

[38] U.S. ground forces (first the Marines and now Army units) have been committed sparingly and only to carry out specific tasks such as clearing particular caves, receiving prisoners, or providing base security.

[39] Michael R. Gordon and General Bernard E. Trainor, USMC (ret), *The Generals' War: The Inside Story of the Conflict in the Gulf*, (Boston: Little, Brown, and Company, 1995), 241. The "palpable skepticism of commando operations" was a carryover from Vietnam. Schwarzkopf's felt that these units were not particularly successful in Southeast Asia and did not acquit themselves well in Grenada. This skepticism manifested itself in Schwarzkopf's belated use of these units in the Scud hunt during the Gulf War.

operation. Support of foreign insurgents is not a new concept; yet, our current joint doctrine addresses this support from a Cold War era insurgency and foreign internal defense (counterinsurgency) slant with a distinctly special forces flavor. These operations have typically worn a clandestine veil and have yielded mixed results. In our doctrine, the term "surrogate" appears only tangentially within the definition of "unconventional warfare" as a SOF principle mission.[40]

Joint Publication (JP) 3-05, *Doctrine for Joint Special Operations*, and JP 3-07.1, *Joint Tactics, Techniques and Procedures for Foreign Internal Defense (FID)*, outline the FID operational framework and tenets. JP 3-07.1 defines FID as "participation by civilian and military agencies of a government in any of the action programs taken by another government to free and protect its society from subversion, lawlessness, and insurgency."[41] It involves all elements of national power and can occur across a broad range of military operations. These operations are typically joint in nature and support strategic and operational goals.[42] Normally, SOF receives FID missions due to their unique training, organization, and regional focus; however, in many cases, these operations require joint planning and preparation to

---

[40] Unconventional Warfare – organize, train, equip, advise, and assist indigenous and surrogate forces in military and paramilitary operations normally of long duration. See *United States Special Operations Forces Posture Statement 2000*, 43.

[41] U.S. Joint Chiefs of Staff, *Joint Tactics, Techniques and Procedures for Foreign Internal Defense (FID)*, Joint Publication 3-07.1, (Washington, D.C.: 26 June 1996), I-1. JP 3-0 speaks more in terms of nations and discusses the considerations for multinational operations, which may or may not involve combat. These considerations include: national goals, unity of effort, doctrine, training, and equipment, cultural differences, management of resources, and national communications. U.S. Joint Chiefs of Staff, *Doctrine for Joint Operations,* Joint Publication 3-0, (Washington, D.C.: 1 February 1995), VI-2. These factors interact with other considerations during the planning and execution of multinational operations (rules of engagement, the media, local law enforcement, command and control, intelligence, logistics, and protection) to generate a complex and dangerous environment. See also page VI-5.

[42] U.S. Joint Chiefs of Staff, *Doctrine for Joint Special Operations,* Joint Publication 3-05, (Washington, D.C.: 17 April 1998), II-7.

ensure that all of the service and functional components are mutually supportive and focused.[43]

FID is further subdivided into indirect support, direct support (not combat operations), and combat operations to support host nation efforts.[44] U.S. intelligence, logistic, and civil-military support might fall under the category of direct operations while combat operations might involve U.S. forces supporting the host nation in its fight against insurgents or terrorists. The flavor of the combat relationship between the U.S. and its theater ground force that was alluded to in Kosovo and exists today in Afghanistan is notably absent from this doctrine.

JP 3-0 defines two critical terms: alliances and coalitions. Alliances are built using formal agreements with broad, long-term objectives. Coalitions, on the other hand, are ad hoc arrangements for a common action.[45] JP 3-0 points out, "As long as the coalition members perceive their membership and participation as advancing their individual national interests, the coalition can remain intact. At the point that national objectives or priorities diverge, the coalition breaks down."[46] The ongoing operation in Afghanistan is clearly multinational; however, it departs from a strictly FID operation. Our relationship with the anti-Taliban forces is an ad hoc coalition for a very specific common action. As JP 3-0 predicted, we may be witnessing the divergence of individual priorities within this coalition. None of these joint documents, however, prescribe how to integrate this surrogate force into our own joint warfighting dynamic.

---

[43] Department of the Army, *Operations*, FM 3-0, 9-8.

[44] From an Army perspective, foreign internal defense (FID) falls under the category of stability operations. Stability operations are intended "to promote and protect U.S. national interests by influencing the threat, political, and informational dimensions of the operational environment." Such operations might include developmental and cooperative activities or, if necessary, coercive actions with the ultimate goal of promoting global or regional stability. See Ibid., 9-1.

[45] U.S. Joint Chiefs of Staff, *Doctrine for Joint Operations,* JP 3-0, VI-1.

[46] Ibid.

VI. The Modern U.S. Insurgency

A. The Surrogate Army

> *The American Special Forces have been ordering airstrikes. Then,*
> *when the area is clear, they are saying to us 'Come, take this place.'*
>
> An aide to a top Pashtun tribal leader[47]

The most far-reaching departure of this surrogate army paradigm from other insurgencies and our joint doctrine lies its integration as a primary force multiplier. For the most part, insurgencies and operations with foreign governments have been "relegated to peripheral field manuals" while primary ground doctrine focused on the "Active Defense" or the "Air-Land Battle."[48] Lately, international coalitions have received a lot of attention; however, this often has been to obtain United Nations' sanction and to gain legitimacy for U.S. actions. Surrogate army doctrine lies between the out-dated, Soviet-threat, land wars and the ethereal low-intensity conflicts and peacekeeping missions.

The means to put this surrogate concept into application requires a different set of conditions than past conflicts, which may have existed under the cloak of insurgency or counterinsurgency. From the onset, we must recognize the conditions that would warrant a surrogate. As previously mentioned, ground conflicts rooted in religious, cultural, or ethnic enmities are a prime backdrop for surrogate operations. Within this theater, there must be an indigenous force with the will to fight (and whom we can leverage to our gain). While few

---

[47] Rajiv Chandrasekaran and John Pomfret, "Aided By U.S., Pashtun Militias Move Closer To Kandahar," *Washington Post*, 27 November 2001, 6, <http://ebird.dtic.mil/Nov2001/e20011127aided.htm> [28 November 2001].

[48] John T. Fishel, "Little Wars, Small Wars, LIC, OOTW, The GAP, and Things That Go Bump in the Night," Naval War College Reprint from *Low Intensity Conflict and Law Enforcement*, vol. 4, no. 3, Winter 1995 issue, 385.

nations invest in air and sea forces, almost all have armies, land-based paramilitary, or police forces.[49] Given their appropriate commitment, these are our surrogates. Finally, this indigenous force must be legitimate in the eyes of the local population. If such support appears to be lacking, then the U.S. must revisit the root causes of the conflict and discover why the majority of the population appears to be content with the existing regime.

Perhaps one of the more unique aspects of surrogate army doctrine is its integration into the joint planning requirements while not becoming an explicit member of the joint force. When faced with an international conflict, our National Command Authority assembles components from the political, economic, informational, and military realms.[50] As General Shelton has written, "Never before has the need for closer collaboration between military leaders and diplomatic community been more crucial."[51] To this end, our diplomatic corps assembles its international coalitions while our military forces draw assets from across the combined arms spectrum to maximize the application of our national power. Our surrogate army straddles these two pillars. Once identified, the surrogate army enjoys the unique position of executing solely on a tactical and operational level. The strategic decision making occurs within the U.S. joint force. The warfighting CINC must channel these plans to the surrogate force in a manner that will preserve the surrogate's decision-making integrity and honor while yielding the U.S.'s desired end state.

---

[49] Department of the Army, *Operations*, FM 3-0, 9-3.

[50] Political assets include: The President, Department of State, CIA, Congress, and the Department of Justice. Economic assets include: the Treasury, Department of Commerce, U.S. aid, and the Peace Corps. Informational assets include the National Security Agency and Public Affairs officers. Military assets include the various services and their individual components, but in particular, civil affairs (CA) and PSYOPS units.

[51] Shelton, 77.

As with all conflicts, the means to affect the ends is driven by the strategic objective. In today's global environment, that effort will be, on some level, joint, interagency, and even multinational. Our current doctrine applauds *unity of command* as essential in securing one's objective enroute to a desired end state; however, the fragmented nature of current multinational land combatants makes this principle extremely elusive.[52] Each player, therefore, must endeavor toward *unity of effort* to obtain his or her desired *objective*.[53] Consequently, a surrogate ground force focused by *unity of effort* becomes the requisite force multiplier to maintain relevance in current doctrine. On the battlefield, this effort will be guided by centralized direction from the U.S. and result in decentralized execution by the surrogate.

The U.S. is learning in Afghanistan that maintaining *unity of effort* is easier said than done, and its presence may be fleeting. The U.S. must be able to maintain leverage over the surrogate force. Our goal is to ensure that our surrogate army's objectives continue to complement ours throughout the conflict. This can be accomplished with a "carrot" or a "stick." A "stick," however, is likely to alienate the very soldiers we want to integrate into the joint force. We are, therefore, left with "carrots," typically of a diplomatic or materiel flavor. Materiel "carrots" carry with them the potential side effect of getting in too deep as we did in

---

[52] Fishel, 388. Fishel makes this point in general terms in his article.

[53] *Objective* is a principle of war whose purpose is to direct every military operation toward a clearly defined, decisive object. See JP 3-0, A-1. *Unity of effort* is not a principle of war and requires coordination and cooperation among all forces toward a commonly recognized objective, although they are not necessarily part of the same command structure. See JP 3-0, A-2. *Unity of command* is a principle of war and means having a single commander control all the forces assigned to a particular mission. See Milan N. Vego, *Operational Warfare,* (Naval War College, 2000), 187.

Vietnam and China. Our efforts to maintain leverage must be accomplished diplomatically and with minimal long-term investment as we did in El Salvador.[54]

Our dependence on surrogate armies stems from the destabilized global security environment, the complex nature of regional conflicts, and our aversion to casualties and prolonged conflicts. As mentioned earlier, the concept evolved from insurgency efforts of the past and has been shaped by our desire to minimize collateral damage to the civilian population while aggressively applying combat power. As Colonel Waghelstein, the American military group commander in El Salvador, stated, "if you've got to commit U.S. ground forces to a theater you essentially have already blown it."[55] The context of his statement was vis-à-vis Latin American counterinsurgency efforts. Today, the requirement has evolved. We still require aggressive application of combat power; however, as Kosovo illustrated, ground troops are essential. A surrogate army allows us to satisfy both conditions, but as with any plan, there are pitfalls and problems.

B. Potential Pitfalls and Problems

A half-baked scheme.

Retired Marine General Anthony Zinni[56]

The challenges of employing a surrogate exist through all phases of a conflict. Even before the onset of hostilities, one overarching concern is the surrogate's very nature. Allies

---

[54] Some have speculated that the arrival of our own ground forces into Afghanistan represents an attempt to leverage the future Afghan regime by holding some territory. This carries the risk of placing our own ground troops in an environment we had hoped to avoid. See William M. Arkin, "Dropping 15,000 Pounds of Frustration," *Los Angeles Times*, 15 December 2001, 10.

[55] Waghelstein, 25.

[56] Vince Crawley, "Is Saddam the next focus?" *Army Times*, 3 December 2001, 14. GEN Zinni was referring to current plans to organize an Iraqi opposition force and send it into battle against Saddam.

made for convenience sake may not be great people or savory characters, and Americans should not be surprised to see who we draw on for assistance. Regarding this quandary, General Shelton remarked, "In the war on terrorism, there are lots of organizations that we might not consider to be an ally, or friend or partner. You have to use those tools when and where they are appropriate."[57] The KLA, for example, had a reputation as drug runners, black marketeers, and by some accounts, terrorists. With the Northern Alliance, there had been reports of pillaging and of Taliban prisoner massacres. Ultimately, the U.S. may find itself forced to protect the local population from their "liberators."[58] Assistant Secretary of State Christina Rocca commented, "The respect for human rights and accountability are part of our message now to the Northern Alliance and have been from the very beginning...we expect human rights to be observed."[59] The U.S. could write off these concerns by applying the Cold War adage, "Yes, they're drug lords, but they're our drug lords."[60] However, one must carefully scrutinize the strength of these coalitions. The Northern Alliance receives backing from a number of sources to include America, Russia, Iran, China, and India, which suggests how many different directions our surrogate army may ultimately be pulled.[61] Along this same vein, switching sides is a common occurrence in Afghan conflicts. The Russians learned this lesson in the 1980s. Missions involving Afghan tribes are delicate ones, and the loyalty of

---

[57] Associated Press, "Shelton: U.S. Will Have Diverse Allies," *MSNBC Website*, 21 October 2001, <http://www.msnbc.com/local/wncn/nbcx7gugxsc.asp> [21 November 2001].

[58] Conrad C. Crane, "D-days in the War on Terrorism," *Strategic Studies Institute Newsletter*, November 2001.

[59] "State Department Cautions Northern Alliance," <http://www.washingtonpost.com/wp-dyn/articles/A21468-2001Nov13 html> [21 November 2001].

[60] Moran.

[61] Ibid.

these forces must always be held in question.[62] Sergei Khrushchev, son of the late Soviet leader Nikita Khrushchev, offers this advice, "You have to know who to support today and who to support tomorrow, but not have enemies and friends. What you have to have is American national interests."[63]

Beyond our surrogate's sense of virtue is their ability to prosecute the war as an effective fighting force. Ideally, the U.S. will discriminate and choose a surrogate army with not only the will but also the capability to fight. This may not always be the case. There is the distinct possibility that a well-armed surrogate will be a poor substitute for proper U.S. military strategy and forces. The Israeli army learned this lesson in the failure of the South Lebanese Army (SLA), their surrogate force in Southern Lebanon.[64] Ultimately, arming friendly insurgents may be a better way of bleeding and punishing enemies than of bringing conflicts to a close.[65]

An additional concern is that the U.S. will sacrifice its primary war fighting ability or mission in pursuit of more unconventional operations alongside foreign forces. General Shelton sees this as a dangerous temptation. He feels the U.S. must "strike a balance" between traditional and non-traditional missions and reminds us that the central purpose of our military

---

[62] Crane.

[63] Siobhan McDonough, "Former Soviet Talks About the War," *The Newport (R.I.) Daily News*, 2 January 2002, B3.

[64] Charles Heyman, "World Armies, Lebanon, Current Developments and Recent Operations," *Jane's Online*, <http://www4.janes.com> [26 November 2001]. The SLA was created by an Israeli reserve Colonel. It was about 2500 strong and consisted of approximately 15 percent Muslims. The SLA operated in the buffer zone between north of Israel and Southern Lebanon. In June 2000, this surrogate force collapsed in the space of two days and forced the Israeli government to order an immediate troop withdrawal. This hasty exodus forced over 6000 Christian and Druze militiamen and their families to flee to Israel. With the Israeli sponsors gone, the SLA disintegrated, and a United Nations force is now patrolling this border. See also Charles Heyman, "World Armies, Lebanon, National Overview," *Jane's Online*, <http://www4.janes.com> [26 November 2001].

[65] Daalder and O'Hanlon, 135.

is "fighting and winning the major conflicts which pose the most serious threats to the United States and its national interest."[66]

The conflict's transition into the post-hostilities phase reveals other challenges. As mentioned earlier, popular support is critical to sustaining indigenous forces and resisting repressive regimes. Consequently, the relationship of the surrogate army to the dominant portion of the population may have lasting implications. In Kosovo, the KLA represented a vast majority of the ethnic Albanian population. In contrast, the Northern Alliance is made up primarily of ethnic Uzbeks and Tajiks. These two groups are a minority of the Afghan population. There was a pervasive fear that unfettered U.S. support of these northern tribes would drive the southern Pashtun tribes back to the Taliban.[67] Fortunately, our careful diplomatic and military contacts have prevented this situation. An additional concern is that the U.S., by choosing a local surrogate, complicates post-hostilities by choosing sides in the conflict. The allies struggled with this dilemma in adopting the KLA in Kosovo whereas NATO did not want to lose their "neutral stance" and still hoped to play a mediating role in Kosovo's political future.[68]

The introduction of U.S. forces poses large force protection problems. As a rule, American troops make "lousy peacekeepers – not because they are not great soldiers but precisely because the are."[69] Our soldiers are lucrative targets both physically and symbolically. Peacekeeping should be left to our allies (as the British are doing in

---

[66] Shelton, 78.

[67] Gordon, "Alliance of Convenience," A1.

[68] Daalder and O'Hanlon, 152. KLA operations were not officially coordinated and occurred largely through a covert CIA relationship to help preserve any chance of neutrality. See Benjamin S. Lambeth, *NATO's Air War For Kosovo: A Strategic and Operational Assessment*, (RAND Corporation, 2001), 72.

Afghanistan), and nation building should be left to the United Nations. Here our surrogate army offers a layer of insulation from the more mundane, but no less dangerous, requirements of a military campaign.

Perhaps the greatest pitfall impacting both combat and post-hostilities is the potential for divergent objectives between surrogate and sponsor. This issue has been raised throughout this paper and calls into question the established allegiances of the players. The final stage of the hunt for Al Qaeda in the Tora Bora Mountains illustrates the division between war aims. The U.S. continues to hunt for Al Qaeda's leaders while our surrogate army begins to reduce pressure on the region.[70] The onset of winter only exacerbates the problem. Many of the opposition forces are poorly clothed, poorly fed, and tired of fighting. From their perspective, the elimination of the Taliban ground forces completes their mission, and they are ready to go home. Additionally, should the Taliban resurface after U.S. forces have left Afghanistan, individuals who "collaborated" with the United States may suffer the political consequences.[71] These issues demonstrate the continued need to find a means to leverage this force and highlight several weaknesses of our surrogate army in Afghanistan.

---

[69] Krauthammer, , 27.

[70] Factions of the Afghan opposition have not pursued the Taliban leaders to the extent the U.S. would have liked. There is continued concern that, once the Taliban has been effectively removed from power, the resistance fighters will begin to withdraw (as some have done in the Tora Bora region). Lately, the Afghan fighters have been more concerned with regaining territory and with expelling Arab and foreign fighters recruited by Al Qaeda. The United States, on the other hand, remains committed to capturing or killing Osama bin Laden. Michael R. Gordon, "One War, Differing Aims," *The New York Times*, 18 December 2001, A1.

[71] Arkin, 10.

VII.   Conclusion

We see, therefore, that war is not merely an act of policy but a true political instrument, a continuation of political intercourse, carried on by other means.

Carl von Clausewitz
On War[72]

Despite changing times and advances in technology, the international community is as complex and embroiled in politics as it has ever been. Our *National Security Strategy* and *National Military Strategy* both adjust to face the conditions of global environment and the threat therein. Similarly, our military doctrine is a living document that responds to evolving threats, increased commitments, and reduced tolerances for casualties. Most future operations will require a joint force tailored for the task at hand; however, some of our global obligations are so untenable as to give the NCA and military leaders pause in employing substantial U.S. ground forces. The adoption of a surrogate army has become a new facet in the evolution of warfare and offers a means of inserting a ground force into a myriad of environments that otherwise might be denied to U.S. troops. U.S. interests exist on a variety of levels. Some warrant the use of our forces and others do not. NATO's war in Kosovo illustrated the need to have ground troops in theater and highlighted the sentiment that "the leader with troops on the ground ultimately calls the tune."[73] Through a surrogate, the U.S. joint force commander can still meet the military-political goals of the NCA while limiting the number of U.S. soldiers on foreign soil.

---

[72] Carl von Clausewitz, *On War,* Edited by Michael Howard and Peter Paret, (Princeton, New Jersey: Princeton University Press, 1984), 87.

[73] Moran,.

A surrogate is not appropriate for every conflict. Leaders must recognize the conditions that would lead us to the selection of a surrogate. Principally, the U.S. should consider surrogate armies for any international crisis that requires troops on the ground but is embroiled in deep-seeded ethnic and religious differences or applies to our lesser national interests. Interventions on humanitarian grounds, reflecting less than vital interests, are becoming increasingly prevalent, and in many cases, the "introduction of thousands of conventional troops could cause more problems than they might solve."[74] In this environment, the surrogate force must have not only the capability, but also the will to fight. Finally, the surrogate must enjoy some legitimacy in the eyes of the people. They may not need to be ethnically dominant or representative of the population; however, their cause must address the concerns of the population. This will ensure the internal support for the force, help minimize our own force protection threat, and increase the hostility level against the enemy regime. U.S. military power alone cannot achieve lasting success. Further, U.S. military power cannot ensure the survival of regimes that fail to meet their people's basic needs. The host governments must address or revise its polices towards the disaffected portions of the population.[75] These were core lessons of past insurgencies, and for the U.S. to emerge successful in surrogate operations, we must be on the proper side of the fence regarding domestic issues. This seemingly clean solution offers new complexities to the joint force commander's operation.

It is quite possible that the U.S. will become involved with a surrogate army that consists of unsavory characters, are lousy fighters, or have divergent objectives (or a

---

[74] Bill Gertz and Rowan Scarborough, "Inside the Ring," *Washington Times*, 11 January 2002, 9.

[75] Department of the Army, *Operations*, FM 3-0, 9-9.

combination thereof). To help mitigate these pitfalls, the operational commander must be able to steer our surrogate using a combination of diplomacy, military advisors, and leverage (be it positive or negative). Our conventional forces will retain a role in achieving this end. Certainly, SOF will maintain an important liaison and training mission; however, there will be expanded rolls for civil affairs and PSYOPS units that extend beyond loudspeakers and flyers. These units will assist in identifying and translating in-country conditions to the warfighters. They must stay in tune with the military aspirations of the surrogate force to help anticipate rifts between U.S. and surrogate interests. Finally, they must remain continuously vigilant for means to leverage the force.

To improve our surrogate's military posture, the U.S. must set the stage for success by isolating our foe. Failing to do so may channel the conflict into the proxy wars of the Cold War era where two powers fight each other indirectly. Even a small amount of support from an enemy sponsor will give our opponent the lift it needs to sustain the fight. We did not isolate our foes in Korea or Vietnam. We were, however, able to do it in Kosovo and Afghanistan.

Military aims will surely diverge. We should anticipate this split and apply active means to keep the force focused. Such means could include all the elements of national power, but our decision-makers must understand what motivates our surrogate in order to harness that motivation to support U.S. interests.

Lastly, to help alleviate the problems of employing a surrogate, the U.S. should not plan on any long-term friendships with our surrogate army. Today's friends are tomorrow's enemies. We must use them to achieve our ends just as they will surely use us to obtain theirs.

Despite any discussions to the contrary, the U.S. will be involved in the global community and will face environments that do not support vital national interests. Our ability to recognize and employ a surrogate army may provide the means to extend our military reach into high risk or inimical foreign environments. It is a new tool for the joint force commander, evolved from past insurgency and proxy war experience, which can play a critical role in winning our future "savage wars of peace."

Bibliography

"Background Note: Afghanistan." *U.S. Department of State Website.* <http://www.state.gov/r/pa/bgn/index.cfm?docid=5380> [21 November 2001].

Associated Press. "Shelton: U.S. Will Have Diverse Allies." *MSNBC Website,* 21 October 2001. <http://www.msnbc.com/local/wncn/nbcx7gugxsc.asp> [21 November 2001].

Byman, Daniel L., Kenneth M. Pollack, and Gideon G. Rose. "Beef Up the Taliban's Enemy." *RAND Op-Eds.* 20 September 2001. <http://www.rand.org/hot/op-eds/092001LAT.html> [21 November 2001].

Clark, Wesley K. *Waging Modern War.* New York: PublicAffairs, 2001.

Clausewitz, Carl von. *On War.* Edited by Michael Howard and Peter Paret. Princeton, New Jersey: Princeton University Press, 1984.

Crane, Conrad C. "D-days in the War on Terrorism." *Strategic Studies Institute Newsletter,* November 2001.

Daalder, Ivo H. and Michael E. O'Hanlon. *Winning Ugly: NATO's War to Save Kosovo.* Washington, D.C.: Brookings Institution Press, 2000.

Department of the Army. *Operations.* Field Manual 3-0. Washington, D.C.: June 2001.

Dreyer, Edward L. *China at War, 1901-1949.* New York: Longman Group Limited, 1995.

Fishel, John T. "Little Wars, Small Wars, LIC, OOTW, The GAP, and Things That Go Bump in the Night." Naval War College Reprint from *Low Intensity Conflict and Law Enforcement,* vol. 4, no. 3, Winter 1995 issue. pp. 372-398.

Gordon, Michael R. and General Bernard E. Trainor, USMC (ret). *The Generals' War: The Inside Story of the Conflict in the Gulf.* Boston: Little, Brown, and Company, 1995.

Heyman, Charles. "World Armies, Lebanon, Current Developments and Recent Operations." *Jane's Online.* <http://www4.janes.com> [26 November 2001].

_____. "World Armies, Lebanon, National Overview." *Jane's Online.* <http://www4.janes.com> [26 November 2001].

Lambeth, Benjamin S. *NATO's Air War For Kosovo: A Strategic and Operational Assessment.* RAND Corporation, 2001.

Moran, Michael. "Uneasy alliance." *MSNBC Website,* 15 November 2001. <http://www.msnbc.com/news/657739.asp#BODY> [21 November 2001].

Shelton, Henry H. "From the Chairman: U.S. Military and Foreign Policy." *Harvard International Review,* vol. XX, no. 1 (Winter 1997/1998): 77-78.

Snider, Michael. "A Quagmire of Alliances and Enmities." *Maclean's*. 8 October 2001. Lexis-Nexis. Dayton, OH: Lexis-Nexis. <http://web.lexis-nxis.com/universe/document?_m=5c0b8097f59ccee3991ea2eac70b46d3&_docnum=39&wchp=dGLStV-lSlAl&_md5=8f46711b35c0c99c9bb39afd261385cc> (21 November 2001).

The White House. *A National Security Strategy for a Global Age*. Washington, D.C.: December 2000.

U.S. Joint Chiefs of Staff. *Doctrine for Joint Operations*. Joint Publication 3-0. Washington, D.C.: 1 February 1995.

_____. *Doctrine for Joint Special Operations*. Joint Publication 3-05. Washington, D.C.: 17 April 1998.

_____. *Joint Tactics, Techniques and Procedures for Foreign Internal Defense (FID)*. Joint Publication 3-07.1. Washington, D.C.: 26 June 1996.

_____. *Unified Action Armed Forces*. Joint Publication 0-2. Washington, D.C.: 10 July 2001.

Office of the Assistant Secretary of Defense (Special Operations/Low-Intensity Conflict). *United States Special Operations Forces Posture Statement 2000*. Washington, D.C.: 2000.

Vego, Milan N. *Operational Warfare*. Naval War College, 2000.

Waghelstein, John D. *El Salvador*. Carlisle Barracks, PA: U.S. Army Military History Institute, Senior Officers Oral History Program, 1985

_____. *Preparing for the Wrong War: the United States Army and Low Intensity Conflict 1755-1890*. Ph.D. Dissertation, 1990.

Warren, David. "America's Advantage." *DavidWarrenOnline*. Essays on Our Times. 12 December 2001. <davidwarrenonline.com> [17 December 2001].